MARCEL FEIGEL AND BRIAN BUSSELLE

The HIGH ANXIETY DIET

AND OTHER ANXIOUS WAYS TO SUCCESS

DRAWINGS BY BILL KERWIN

Andrews and McMeel
A Universal Press Syndicate Company
Kansas City • New York

The High Anxiety Diet
Copyright © 1990 by Marcel Feigel

All rights reserved. Printed in the United States of America. No part of this book may be used or reproduced in any manner whatsoever without written permission except in the case of reprints in the context of reviews. For information write Andrews and McMeel, A Universal Press Syndicate Company, 4900 Main Street, Kansas City, Missouri 64112.

ISBN: 0-8362-2413-2

Library of Congress Catalog Card Number: 89-82510

First published in Great Britain in 1988 by
Frederick Muller, an imprint of Century Hutchinson Ltd.
Brookmount House, 62-65 Chandos Place
London WC2N 4NW

ATTENTION: SCHOOLS AND BUSINESSES

Andrews and McMeel books are available at quantity discounts with bulk purchase for educational, business, or sales promotional use. For information, please write to: Special Sales Department, Andrews and McMeel, 4900 Main Street, Kansas City, Missouri 64112.

First Printing, March 1990
Second Printing, April 1990

CONTENTS

Getting into the Stress Habit 9
Stress and Fitness 17
Stress at the Office 27
Love Is 37
In the Wee Small Hours 47
Advanced Stress 51
Life's Little Gifts to Stress Lovers . 63
Recommended Professions 73
Modern Stress 81
What to Read 91
What to Watch 91
Famous People Who Have
    Benefitted from Stress 95
Double Trouble 99
The High Anxiety Diet 105

HOW TO TURN A NAIL-BITING LIFESTYLE INTO A SLIMMER, MORE SUCCESSFUL YOU

FEATURING THE HIGH ANXIETY DIET
THE FIRST DIET THAT LETS YOU EAT AS MUCH AS YOU LIKE

Never mind what you've been told.

Far from being bad for you, anxiety is really your *secret* friend.

A friend who can help you unlock the secrets of success.

This book will show you how.

Starting with simple, everyday anxiety, you will progress to stress in the office, in the bedroom and even during yoga classes.

Once you've mastered the basic stress techniques, you will then graduate to the complex world of advanced anxiety.

And as an added bonus you'll learn how stress can keep you beautifully slim through THE HIGH ANXIETY DIET, the first diet that lets you eat as much as you like as long as you worry about it.

In short, here is everything you need to know to turn panic into a successful lifestyle.

WHY STRESS IS GOOD FOR YOU

We're always told how people "suffer" from stress, as if it were some terrible disease.

Or we read about stress related illness when doctors can't find any other reason for whatever's wrong.

But we're never told about the good that stress does.

After all, life without stress would be placid.

Or worse, complacent (the very word feels like flopping down in an easy chair ready for a full evening of viewing).

Or worst of all, smug.

Stress on the other hand is dynamic.

Stress keeps you on your toes, drives you into action, makes you an achiever and can keep you slim (smugness won't keep you slim, that's for sure).

The trouble is people have been taught to be afraid of stress so they try to avoid it. They run away from it. All this does is create angst and angst is where all the trouble comes from.

The answer lies not just in accepting stress but in embracing it whole-heartedly and letting its magic work for you.

By developing a vigorous "hands on" approach to stress, by becoming a stress *seeker*, you develop dynamic tension that in turn releases a flood of positive energy.

By learning to love stress you will have all that radiant energy at your command.

What's more, anxiety—your secret friend—will be watching and guiding you through the slings and arrows of life.

For the anxious, the world is full of riches. And it's getting wealthier every day.

Never has there been so much to worry about. And the beauty of it is that all that worry can work to your benefit.

All you have to do is say "Yes" to stress.

IF I HAD KNOWN THIS WAS GOING TO BE ON I WOULD HAVE BOUGHT CHEESECAKE

COMPLACENT V ANXIOUS

Wakes up as soon as the alarm rings and jumps out of bed.	Wakes up before the alarm, but doesn't get out of bed until long after it's rung.
Eats slowly, often at the same place.	Eats quickly, sometimes standing up. Often gulps because he's in a hurry, or out of habit.
Books vacations 6 months in advance.	Books the day before and then worries about whether he's going to the right terminal.
Relaxed about the future.	Terrified.
Always finishes what he starts.	Starts numerous projects then gives up halfway through.
Gave up cigarettes a year ago.	Gives them up every month.
Always answers yes when asked at rock concerts if he feels "all right."	Doesn't go to rock concerts because they're always sold out by the time he gets around to them.
Is rarely overdrawn.	Has two overdrafts (both of which he's trying to extend), Mastercard, American Express, VISA and a cash-flow account which is never in credit.
Always leaves his keys and wallet in the exact same place so he can find them immediately.	Usually a desperate, last-minute scramble to find them. Or leaves the house quite contentedly only to return five minutes later in a panic.
Stays with the same partner all his life but fantasizes about other women.	Changes partners regularly and fantasizes about his first grade teacher.

GETTING INTO THE STRESS HABIT

MAKING LISTS

One of the best ways of developing a general level of anxiety is by making lists.

Be sure to make one every day. And leave nothing out. Nothing is too trivial to include, birthday cards to distant cousins, phoning the restaurant to see if they still have your umbrella—throw it all in. The longer the list the better.

And always be sure to add a few too many items (for you must never actually go through the list).

It's also good to include one or two long-range items. So after:

>   Take shirts to cleaners
>   Pick up pint of milk
>   Buy condoms

You can add:

>   Learn French

You've probably wanted to learn French for some time and haven't done anything about it. And you probably won't do anything about it today, but seeing it on the list day after day is a good way to activate a little guilt.

THE MISPLACED WALLET

When you go to bed at night, place your wallet in a pocket where you normally wouldn't put it.

Next morning, when you hit your first financial port of call, you'll instinctively reach for the pocket where you normally keep it. Seeing it's not there, your blood pressure will quickly double its normal rate; your heartbeat will shoot up to an aerobic level roughly equal to running eight miles in two minutes, and you may even hyperventilate.

At the same time your hands will be going through their motions almost as if they have a life of their own.

This is an excellent way of getting a quick burst of High Anxiety. But it's not recommended for newcomers as it can sometimes be fatal.

An interesting variation can be performed with your keys.

THE TAXI

Arrange to have lunch with an old friend, preferably someone you haven't seen for some time. And give yourself just enough time to make it if you hurry and everything goes exactly right which includes getting a taxi the *second* you leave the building.

The chances are that you'll get stuck in heavy midtown traffic. This is beneficial in two ways. On the one hand you're anxious about the time that's slipping away which is particularly useful for breaking up cholesterol around the arteries.

But that anxiety is compounded by the relentless ticking of the meter to remind you that you're losing money in the bargain. This helps release carbohydrates because your anxiety is working in overdrive.

Once you finally get to your destination, you'll probably have a great deal to talk about which will cut fairly deeply into your lunch hour and necessitate another taxi (this is known as "the double taxi"). And that's when the pounds really come rolling off.

Calorie Loss
The taxi   400 calories
The double taxi   900 calories

LEAVING THINGS UNTIL THE LAST MINUTE

Your stress level, like your sugar level, can easily go down, especially at night.

That's why it's important to recharge it in the morning. One of the best ways to get it soaring is by getting a late start and then having to rush.

In stress terms this is the equivalent of the healthy breakfast. Because it sets you up for the rest of the day.

Once procrastination becomes part of your routine you'll wonder how you ever managed without it. And you'll find that it slots neatly into different parts of your life—from arriving late at airports to starting your Christmas shopping at the last minute.

LISTENING TO OTHER PEOPLE'S PROBLEMS

People are always ready to tell you their troubles, especially when you don't have time to listen. They have an uncanny ability to catch you just as you're going somewhere.

Because they get very easily offended, your only choice is either to listen attentively or patiently explain that though you haven't got the time this second, you'd be happy to get together some other time when you could really discuss the situation in depth.

Either way you get a workout.

Listening to the problems of others especially when you do it out of politeness, while appearing concerned, fuels a slow burning anxiety that's all the more effective because it can't be seen.

THE ANXIOUS PHONE CALL

VISITING THE BANK MANAGER

STRESS AND FITNESS

Let's be honest, anxiety alone can only do so much. If you really want to stay trim then you must exercise.

And here we come to the best of both worlds – anxious exercise.

For if exercise tones the body, sharpens the mind and helps you burn up calories, then just think of the fantastic results you can achieve by *worrying while you exercise*.

RON'S GETTING SUSPICIOUS OF ALL THIS JOGGING...
YES, SO'S BEATRICE.
DAILY EXPRESS
PROMINENT BUSINESS MAN DIES ON MORNING JOG

AEROBICS

YOGA

Yoga is an ideal exercise for anxious people because it gives you the most time to worry.

It's particularly useful for slimming and is recommended as part of the High Anxiety Diet.

Never mind what yoga instructors say about clearing the mind and letting tension float away — that's just a fad which probably started in LA.

It's true there are some Swamis who advocate stressless yoga, but have you seen them? Most are definitely on the chubby side.

There is no reason why yoga and worry can't go together. After all, they have for over two thousand years. It's what the Indians call Lean Yoga, now sometimes referred to as Yuppie Yoga. But whatever you call it, it can go a long way to make you the Skinny Minny you always wanted to be.

SHE'S BEEN HAVING QUITE A FEW HEADACHES LATELY...

DEEP RELAXATION

All yoga exercises end with deep relaxation. This is a good time to get to grips with your deepest worries.

One of the best things about anxiety is that it doesn't have to be recent. You can reach back as far as you like and draw on buried neurosis to help you release buried fat.

Remember how your classmates used to pick on you because you were no good at sports. Or the way you never gave yourself any respect because nobody else did. And how no one used to go out with you more than twice and you thought it was just because of your spots. Well, bring it all out, visualizing everything as vividly as if it were yesterday and feel that lithe, head-turning figure, that's always been there trying to get out, becoming a reality.

Calorie Loss
150 Calories

STRESS AT THE OFFICE

Offices can be very anxious places.

Either you're on your way up which is bound to be stressful because you can be sure there will be people trying to block your way.

Or you're on the way down which is even more stressful.

Or you're in the middle, not sure of which way you're going, if you're going anywhere. This can also be fraught with tension.

On the other hand, you could be in a very quiet office where there isn't much happening.

In which case you're really in trouble, because that's the most stressful of all.

ARRIVING LATE FOR A MEETING

ASKING FOR A RAISE

FINDING YOUR NAME REMOVED FROM THE DOOR

SPECULATING WITH COMPANY FUNDS

Calorie Loss
2000 calories

CAUGHT OUT AT YANKEE OR SHEA STADIUM

STARTING AN AFFAIR WITH THE CLIENT'S WIFE

ENDING AN AFFAIR WITH THE CLIENT'S WIFE

WRITING OFF THE COMPANY CAR

RUNNING YOUR OWN COMPANY FROM THE OFFICE

LOVE IS...

A CONSTANT WORRY!

GIVING BUT NOT EXPECTING

$150.00 !!!
THIS BETTER BE WORTH IT.

GIVING PLEASURE

TOTAL TRUST

I ONLY SAID BRUCE "MIGHT" BE BACK...

EVER HOPEFUL

DOES HE TAKE TEA?

BEING THE PERFECT GENTLEMAN

FULL OF SURPRISES

IS BLIND

KNOWING YOUR HEART BELONGS TO JUST ONE PERSON

Calling out the wrong name in bed, either in your sleep or during the height of sexual abandon, can be extremely useful. Because it's a dramatic way of stimulating post-coital anxiety which can offset the giddy relaxation that too often follows sex.

It can also stimulate some fairly heated pillow talk; that is, if the pillows are still there.

But best of all, it will lead to an anxious relationship which is an indispensable part of any true stress seeker's life.

Perhaps you're fortunate in having an anxious relationship already. Or you may even have several. If so, then you're in luck. If you don't, then what are you waiting for? There are plenty to go around.

So why should you feel deprived when it can do such wonderful things for your figure.

Calorie Loss
In your sleep   250 calories
In the throes of passion   600 calories

ADMITTING YOUR SHORTCOMINGS

WE'D BOTH LIKE TO APOLOGIZE

IN THE WEE SMALL HOURS

(NIGHT-TIME ANXIETY)

Nocturnal anxiety follows a path of its own.

Finally freed from the grind of the daily run-around, you can now lie in bed, wide awake, counting your worries instead of sheep.

First get the minor worries out of the way. This allows you to get to grips with deeper, more brooding anxieties.

The ones that, like vampires, only come out at night.

I'VE BEEN IN BED FOR HALF AN HOUR
AND I'M STILL AWAKE!
12·30
THE KIDS AREN'T HOME YET
I WONDER IF ANYTHING'S HAPPENED?
1·00AM
THESE BANK STATEMENTS
AREN'T LOOKING TOO HEALTHY.
STATEMENT
O.D.
O.D.
O.D.
O.D.
O.D.
WHAT HAVE I REALLY ACHIEVED
WITH MY LIFE?
5·00 AM

49

OH, MY GOD, I'M GOING TO BE LATE FOR ANOTHER MEETING!!!
BBBZZZZZEEEEEEE
7:30 AM
ZZZZZ

ADVANCED STRESS

    As you adjust to your new lifestyle, you may find that you need a regular, concentrated dose of high anxiety to maintain the momentum, just like some people grow to need a high fiber diet.
    If that's the case, then you might have to make some changes in your life like...

INVITING THE IN-LAWS FOR THE WEEKEND

GOING FREELANCE

One of the best ways of ensuring an uninterrupted worry flow is by going freelance.

Because the beauty of freelance is that not only do you not know when you're going to get your next job, but you don't know when you're going to get paid for the last one either.

If you're not in a position to go freelance then you may just have to settle with changing jobs.

MOVING

AND GETTING A DIVORCE

In stress terms, both moving and getting a divorce are classics, and can take their place besides other classics like forgetting to claim your lottery prize, losing the matches with the phone number of the new love of your life, or finding out that your sole client has been bought out by Toshiba.

The beauty of moving and getting a divorce is that they create a total upheaval in your life and, if you're fortunate, one can lead to another.

But if you had to choose, divorce would win simply because its effects last longest. As that sage of stress, Woody Allen, remarked, a wife is only a wife for the duration of marriage. An ex-wife is with you forever.

ASKING THE WORKMEN IF THEY WOULD MIND TURNING THE RADIO DOWN

OPENING A WINE BAR IN IRAN

BUYING A MEDICAL DICTIONARY

Needless to say, anxious people are very anxious about their health.

Skeptics dismiss this as hypochondria. But anxious people know better. They know they're coming down with something. And what's more, it's serious.

Anxious people know that there are no such things as minor ailments or common colds. These are just thin disguises for chronic, potentially degenerative diseases.

After all, today's mole is tomorrow's malignant melanoma.

That's why it's important to get the disease before it gets you. That calls for painstaking medical detective work.

By keeping a medical dictionary by your bedside table you'll be able to spring into action at a second's notice with a full list of terrible but obscure diseases that are notorious for evading medical diagnosis.

In time you will also realize the importance of keeping up with medical journals. Because new illnesses are coming out all the time.

And how can you tell when you've got something if you don't even know what it's called.

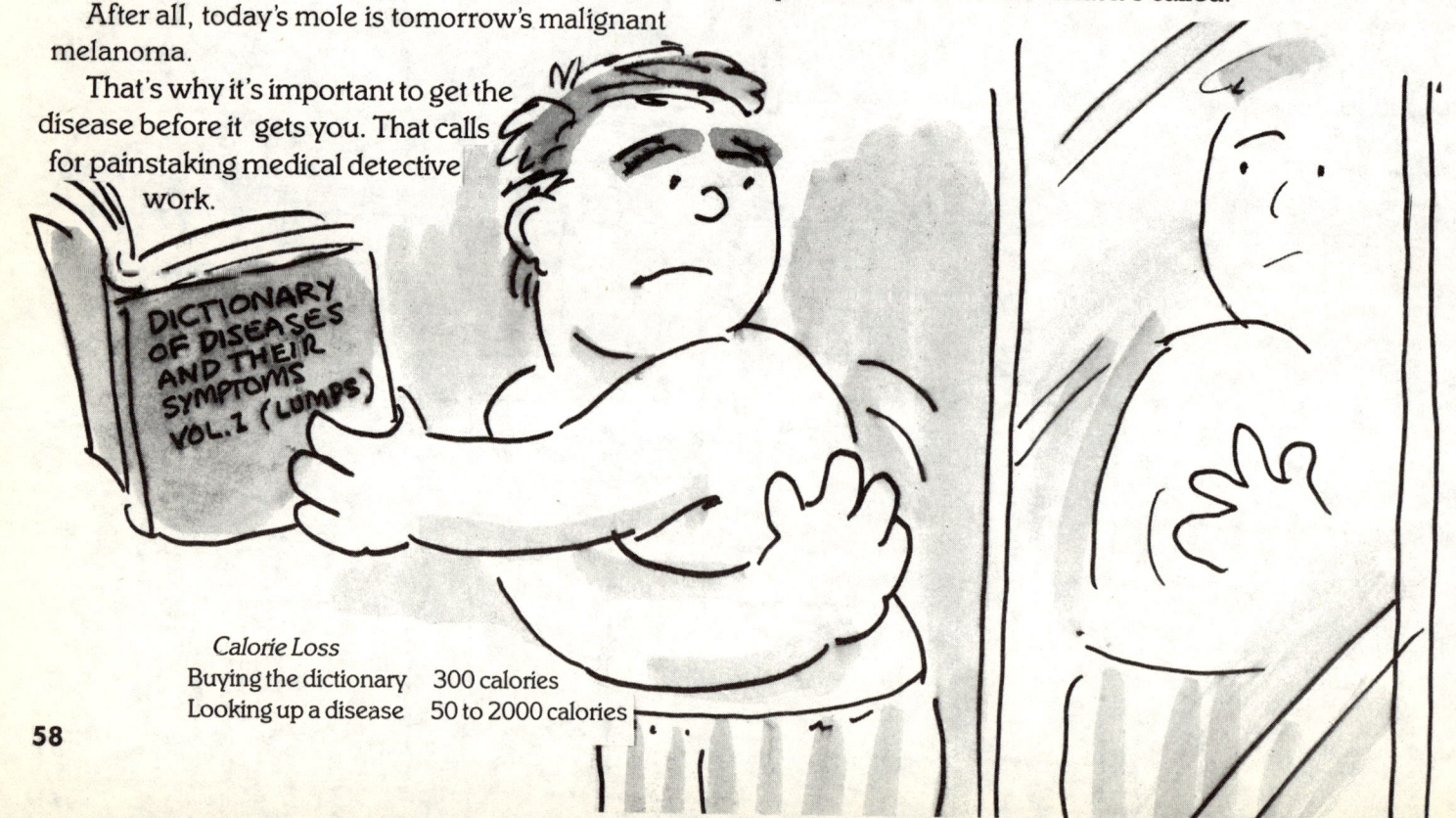

Calorie Loss
Buying the dictionary   300 calories
Looking up a disease   50 to 2000 calories

THROWING A DINNER PARTY FOR PEOPLE WHO DON'T LIKE EACH OTHER

EATING FOOD AFTER THE SELL-BY DATE

NOT PAYING YOUR TAX FOR EIGHT YEARS

MOVING TO NEW YORK

LIFE'S LITTLE GIFTS TO STRESS LOVERS

It's not just the big things that cause anxiety.

Little things are also important, particularly little irritations. These musn't be underestimated, for though minor in impact, these *frissons of friction* play an important part in fueling stress.

Fortunately, modern urban living abounds in irritants, from buses that are 30 minutes late to public telephones that don't work. These all help you sustain a constant stress level.

Another big plus with little irritants is that some of them you can actually buy. Most of these are "convenience" products supposedly designed to make life easier. This is why it makes it even more stressful when they don't work the way they're supposed to.

Some people think the reason you can never find the beginning of a roll of sticky tape or the straw on a juice container is that they've been badly designed. The truth is that manufacturers have come round to recognizing the importance of stress and now build it into their products.

OPENING A BOTTLE OF WINE ON YOUR FIRST DATE.

OPENING A CARTON OF MILK

TRY PULLING IT OUT AND THE WHOLE ROLL COMES TUMBLING OUT.

FINDING THE END OF A ROLL OF SCOTCH TAPE.

GOOD MORNINGS BEGIN

WITH A GOOD

BREAKFAST

EASY TO OPEN JAM JARS.

AW — NUTS!

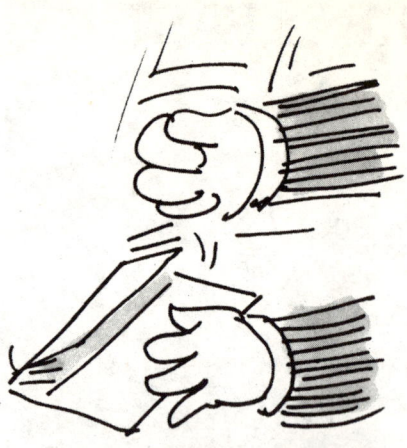

ENVELOPES THAT DON'T STAY STUCK.

WHY DO SHOELACES ALWAYS SNAP WHEN YOU'RE IN A HURRY?

WHERE DID THE STRAW GO?

THE MAP

5

6.

7.

8

9

RECOMMENDED PROFESSIONS

ACCOUNTANT TO THE "FAMILY"

DON.

I DIDN'T EVEN KNOW WE WERE REGISTERED

BOMB DISPOSAL

WAR CORRESPONDENT

DRIVING INSTRUCTOR

STOCKBROKER

LINE CALLER FOR A McENROE MATCH

MODERN STRESS

Like cockroaches and flu germs, stress is infinitely adaptable.

It relishes new situations and thrives on new technology, the more state of the art the better.

Anything new presents a golden opportunity for stress to assert itself. Which is why new strains are being developed every day.

Here are a few that are going around at the moment.

BEING LET DOWN BY YOUR MATE

Calorie Loss
500 calories

LOSING YOUR FILOFAX

THANKS FOR

84

THE MEMORIES

WHEN YOU'RE OUT...

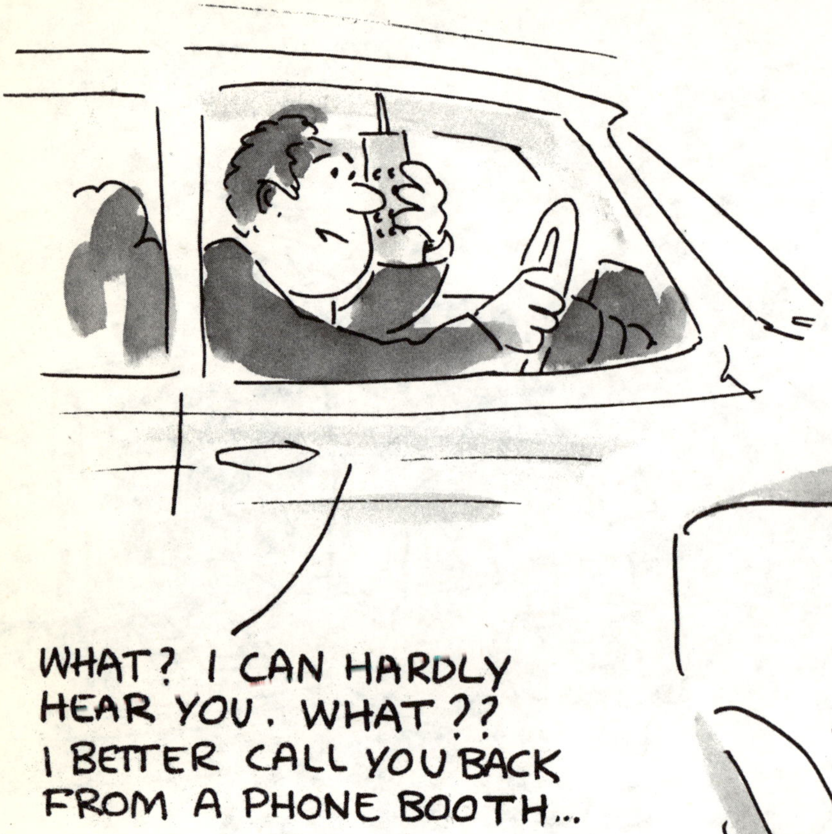

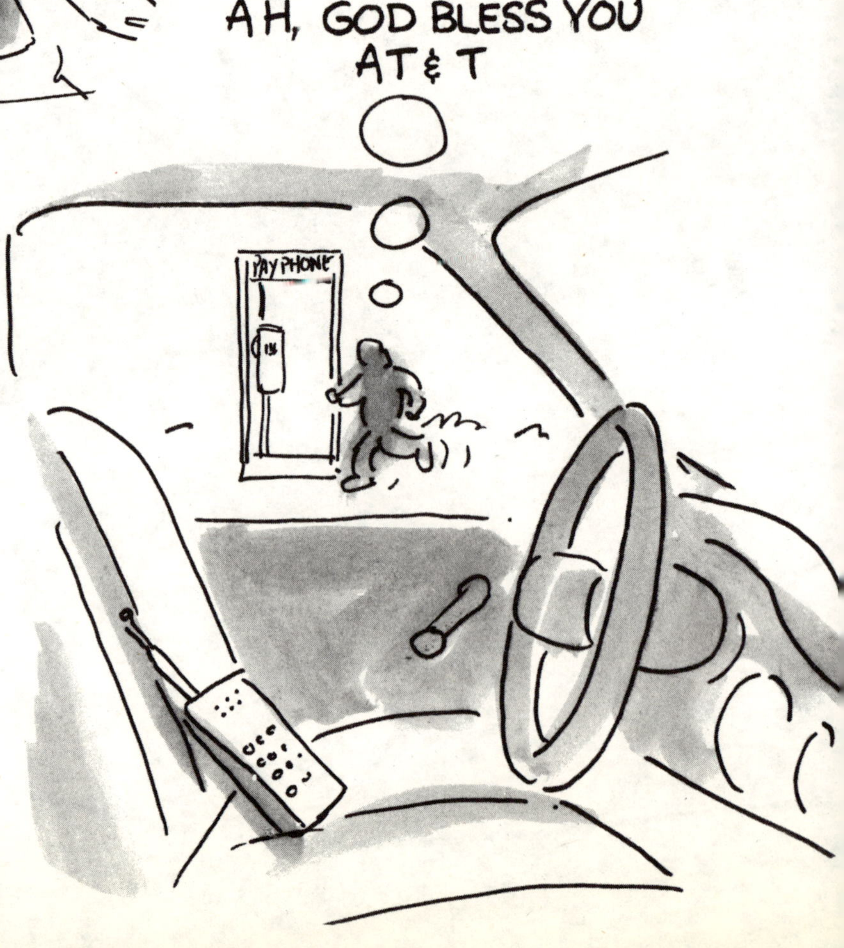

YOU'RE OUT!

TRYING TO REMEMBER WHETHER YOU RECORDED SIXTY MINUTES OVER THE SUPER BOWL

Calorie Loss
700 calories

HAVING A TEENAGER WHO IS ALWAYS PHONING 976 TEEN

LOSING YOUR CONTACT LENSES WHILE HANG GLIDING

WHAT TO READ
WHAT TO WATCH

Required Reading

1. Bank Statements
2. Your children's report cards
3. Bills
4. All documents leaked to *The Washington Post* or *The New York Times*
5. Rejection letters for your gold card applications
6. The Greenpeace Quarterly
7. Anything to do with Dan Quayle becoming president
8. The predictions of Nostradamus
9. Instruction manuals
10. The complete works of Kafka
11. Food labels
12. Novels given by well meaning relatives who say "you must read this."
13. Repeat gift subscriptions to the *Readers Digest*
14. John LeCarre novels after page 20

What to Watch

1. "Sixty Minutes"
2. Nightly News with Ted Koppel
3. Early Chuck Norris films
4. Programs about how the Japanese are buying up America
5. TV evangelists
6. Morton Downey, Jr. reruns
7. Anything to do with AIDS
8. Being forced to watch "The Dating Game" by your teenage daughter
9. Crazy Eddie and Jim Varney commercials
10. 290th repeat of "I Love Lucy"
11. Films like *Psycho*, *Halloween*, and *Midnight Express*
12. Programs on unemployment, world famine, the deterioration of inner cities, the growth of terrorism, the contamination of the earth and Dan Quayle becoming president

FAMOUS PEOPLE WHO HAVE BENEFITTED FROM STRESS

Imelda Marcos
Having to make do in a new country as a deposed dictator's widow with only three truckloads of shoes has kept her young and vigorous.

Mel Brooks
Mr. High Anxiety himself. So impressed was he with this regime that he even made a film about it.

Woody Allen
Did you know that at one time he was fat and not very funny. Until he discovered the joys of stress.

Maggie Thatcher
To look at her you would never think she was addicted to the boxes of chocolate her junior ministers are always leaving her but nevertheless she stays lean and alert. And it's all because the lady loves stress.

Colonel Gaddafy
Going home at night, never knowing if your tent is going to be where you left it, breeds a sense of insecurity which has made him the international sex symbol that he is today.

Nancy Reagan
Acting as the ex-president's cue card is enough to keep anyone cadaverously thin.

Elton John
Worrying about losing your hair while at the same time being anxious about losing your voice has kept him svelte and in top form.

John McEnroe
He used to be known as Mr. Nice Guy in his early days when he was ranked No. 285. Then he discovered stress and his career took off. Though now that he's become a daddy, parental complacency may have set in.

Elizabeth Taylor
How do you think she lost all that weight?

DOUBLE TROUBLE

Just as some vitamins are more effective when combined with others, the same can also be true of stress.

And there is a special breed who prefer their stress in multiple doses — the stronger the better.

These people, who make up a kind of elite, include high powered executives, politicians, Jewish mothers and racing drivers.

But be warned, Double Trouble is definitely not for everybody. The rewards may be great but most people can't stand the strain.

However, once you decide to start doubling up on stress, you'll be pleasantly surprised how easy it is to find.

After a while, you won't even have to look for it. It'll find you.

FALLING IN LOVE WITH A STREET ARTIST WHILE TRYING TO END A RELATIONSHIP WITH A DENTIST

Falling madly in love with someone who is *totally* wrong for you and who you're never sure you'll ever see again is very exciting. It can also be very stressful.

It could be some advertising smoothie you met at a wine bar. Or an actor working as a waiter. Or a pavement artist.

What's exciting – and stressful – is that everything is so uncertain.

Sometimes you may not see him for weeks and just as you're about to finally give him up, he suddenly appears with all the rakish, heartbreaking charm of an Irish poet.

This kind of relationship, if that's what you want to call it, is particularly good for losing weight. And sleep.

But you can become even slimmer if, while worrying about the pavement artist, you're also in the throes of breaking up with a dentist after three (or was it four?) uneventful years.

And you'll lose even more weight if you and he are entangled in a few cumbersome details like co-owning a time-share in Tunisia. And if he still brings his laundry to your flat.

Calorie Loss
750 calories

LISTENING TO YOUR HORSE COME IN LAST IN THE KENTUCKY DERBY AND DRIVING INTO A LAMPPOST

GETTING ON THE WRONG TRAIN THEN DISCOVERING THAT IN YOUR HASTE TO GET OFF YOU LEFT YOUR BRIEFCASE BEHIND

HAVING A JEWISH SON WHO FAILS HIS DOCTOR'S EXAM AND THEN MARRIES A SHIKSA

AND HE LEARNED TO WRITE TO TELL ME THIS!

Dear Mom

Calorie Loss
Failing his doctor's exam   700 calories
Marrying a shiksa   5000 calories

DISCOVERING TWO MONTHS AFTER YOUR MOTHER'S FUNERAL THAT YOUR FATHER HAS MARRIED A 24-YEAR-OLD BIMBO TO WHOM HE PLANS TO LEAVE HIS ENTIRE FORTUNE

THE HIGH ANXIETY DIET

THE MOST REVOLUTIONARY WEIGHT REDUCING IDEA OF OUR TIME

The High Anxiety Diet is the very first diet that lets you eat as much as you like.

No, your eyes didn't deceive you, we said as much as you like — of anything you like.

From cherry trifle to banana splits, deep dish supreme pizzas to croissants with butter and jam, you can have it all.

That's what makes The High Anxiety Diet not just a radical idea, but the most revolutionary weight reducing concept of our time.

Of course there is one *little* proviso.

You've got to worry. Most of your worrying will be done before eating, though it probably wouldn't hurt if you worried a little afterwards as well.

Naturally, the more you eat the more you'll have to worry.

And it shouldn't come as a total surprise to hear that you'll have to worry more after a double cheeseburger and french fries than you would after a cottage cheese salad with rice cakes.

That's only logical. And the laws of anxiety are nothing if not logical.

So with the battle of the bulge, as with so many of life's conflicts, anxiety can be your ally.

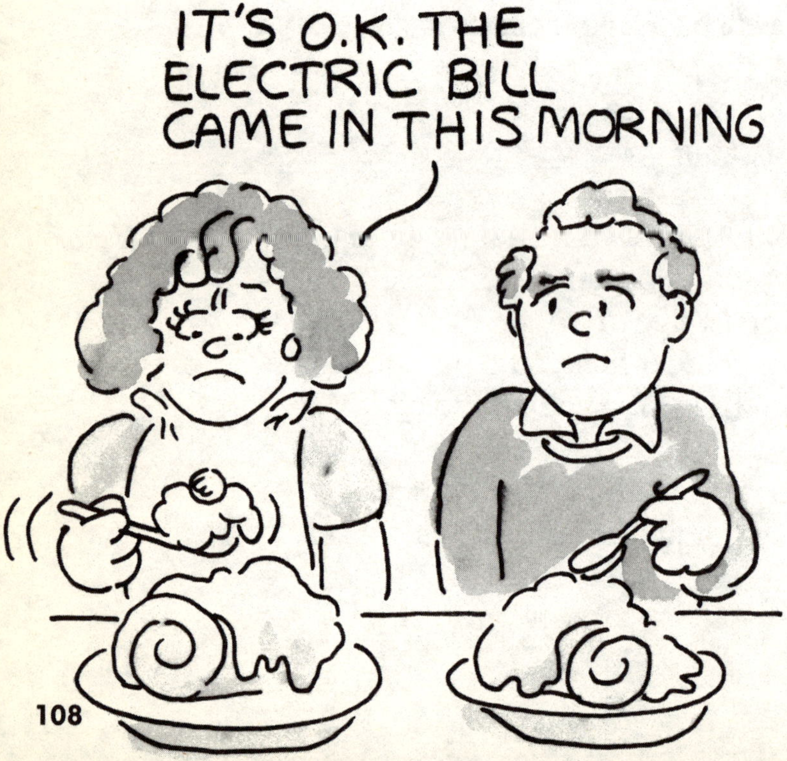
IT'S O.K. THE
ELECTRIC BILL
CAME IN THIS MORNING

CALORIE CHART

CALORIE RATING	FORM OF ANXIETY	REWARD	CALORIE RATING	FORM OF ANXIETY	REWARD
1—100	Thinking about your next visit to the dentist	2 M&M's	1000—1250	Remortgaging your house and starting an affair with your client's wife	German sausage with potato salad and cabbage
100—200	Leaving your new umbrella on the bus	Half a chocolate bar	1250—1500	Not declaring tax	Two stick shish kebab and rice with five glasses of Ouzo and Turkish delight
200—300	Eating frozen shrimp 7 days after the sell-by date	Glazed donut	1500—1800	Not declaring tax and getting a letter from IRS	Two fried eggs, bacon, sausage, home fries, toast and blueberry pancakes with maple syrup
300—450	Leaving for work without checking that the gas is turned off	Eclair	1800—2000	Moving to New York with no contacts	Assorted stuffed bagels with potato latkes
450—600	Spending $100 on a date and not getting anywhere	Banana split	2000—2100	Speculating with company funds	Madras curry with rice, three stuffed parathas, and two large glasses of Lowenbrau
600—1000	Forgetting your wedding anniversary and discovering you've been left out of your father's will	Paté and toast washed down with 2 bottles of wine			

CALORIE RATING	FORM OF ANXIETY	REWARD	CALORIE RATING	FORM OF ANXIETY	REWARD
2100–2200	Going freelance and eating prawns after sell-by date	Deep pan pizza and large Coke	2350–2500	Forgetting to collect winning lottery ticket followed by anxious sex	Roast rib of beef with gravy, mashed potatoes, sauteed brussel sprouts, popovers and chocolate mousse
2200–2250	Being discovered in bed with somebody else by your partner	Bowl of borscht, chicken Kiev and bottle of Bolla	2500–3000	Starting your Christmas shopping at 4:30 on Dec 24 and suspecting that the mole on your neck might be malignant	Saddle of rabbit stuffed with a veal farci, pistachio and pine nuts served with juniper berry sauce flavored with gin and Irish coffee
2250–2300	Moving	Stuffed hogshead in apple sauce followed by fudge brownies	3000–5000	Losing your filofax, your spouse and your biggest client all on the same day	7 course blowout featuring "The Works" including champagne, unlimited wine, stilton and vintage port
2300–2350	Taking the family for a sailing holiday after writing off the company car	Halfpound cheeseburger, large fries, thick chocolate milkshake and apple pie a la mode			

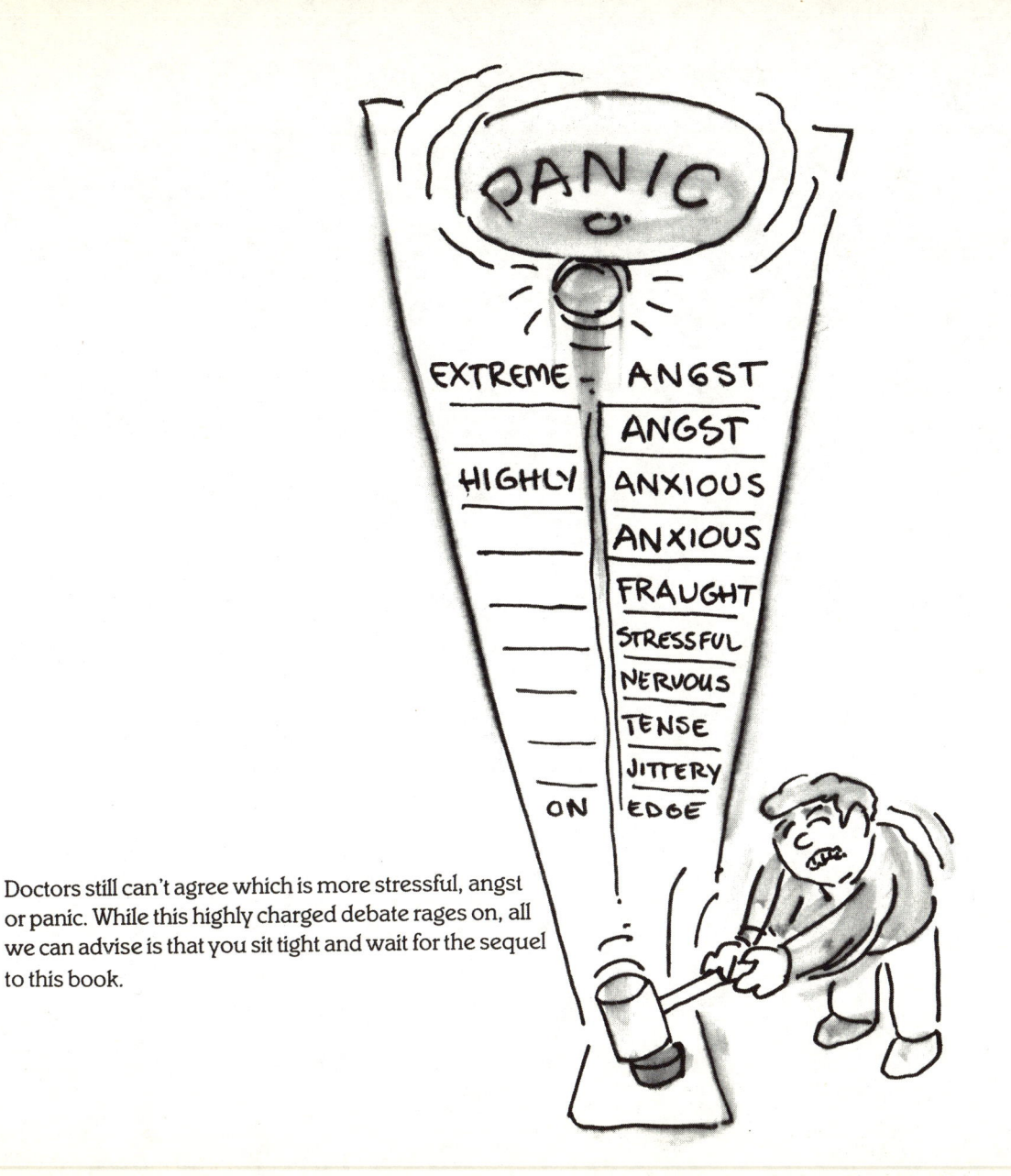

Doctors still can't agree which is more stressful, angst or panic. While this highly charged debate rages on, all we can advise is that you sit tight and wait for the sequel to this book.